Little Big Giant

Stories of Wisdom and Inspiration

Will Smith

Fresh Prince to Hollywood Royalty

Copyright © 2024 Little Big Giant

No part of this publication may be reproduced, stored in a retrieval system, or transmitted in any form or by any means, electronic, mechanical, photocopying, recording, or otherwise, without the prior written permission of the publisher.

Printed in the United States of America

First Edition: 2024

This copyright page includes the necessary copyright notice, permissions request information, acknowledgments for the cover design, interior design, and editing, as well as the details of the first edition.

www.littlebiggiant.com

Disclaimer: This book is a work of non-fiction and is intended for informational and educational purposes only. The names in this biography are trademarks of their respective owners. This book is not affiliated with, endorsed by, or sponsored by any of these trademark holders. The use of these names is intended solely to provide context and historical reference.

The author makes no claims to ownership of any trademarks or copyrights associated with the names and likenesses of the individuals referenced in this book. Any opinions expressed in this book are those of the author and do not reflect the views of any wrestling promotion or trademark holder.

Introduction

As the sun set over the bustling city of Philadelphia, a young Will Smith stood on the corner of 52nd and Market Street, his heart racing with excitement. He had just finished filming his first music video with his best friend, DJ Jazzy Jeff, and the adrenaline was still coursing through his veins.

But little did he know, this was just the beginning of a journey that would lead him to become one of the most iconic and beloved actors of our time.

From his humble beginnings as a rapper, to his breakout role in the hit TV show "The Fresh Prince of Bel-Air," Will Smith's rise to fame was meteoric. But it wasn't without its challenges.

Despite his undeniable talent and charm, Smith faced constant rejection and criticism in Hollywood. But he refused to give up, and his perseverance paid off when he landed the lead role in the blockbuster film "Independence Day."

From there, he continued to captivate audiences with his dynamic performances in films like "Men in Black," "Ali," and "The Pursuit of Happyness." But it wasn't just his acting skills that made him a household name.

Will Smith's infectious personality and genuine love for his fans made him a beloved figure around the world. He used his platform to spread positivity and inspire others to chase their dreams, earning him the title of "America's Favorite Son."

But behind the glitz and glamour of Hollywood, there were also moments of heartache and struggle for Will Smith. From his tumultuous relationship with his first wife, to the tragic loss of his father, he faced his fair share of hardships.

Yet through it all, he remained resilient and continued to push boundaries, becoming the first actor in history to have eight consecutive films gross over $100 million at the box office.

So as the world watched in awe as Will Smith received his star on the Hollywood Walk of Fame, one thing was clear - this was just the beginning for the man who had captured our hearts and inspired us all.

But what lies ahead for Will Smith? Only time will tell, but one thing is for sure - his journey is far from over.

Table of Contents

Table of Contents..9
Chapter 1..11
A Boy from West Philadelphia................................11
Chapter 2..22
The Birth of DJ Jazzy Jeff and The Fresh Prince....22
Chapter 3..34
The Rise of The Fresh Prince of Bel-Air.................34
Chapter 4..46
From Music to Movies: Will Smith's Hollywood Breakthrough..46
Chapter 5..57
Facing Rejection and Overcoming Challenges.......57
Chapter 6..69
The Box Office King: Will Smith's Blockbuster Success..69
Chapter 7..81
A Family Man: Will Smith's Personal Life and Relationships...81

Chapter 8..**92**
The Pursuit of Happiness: Will Smith's Inspirational Journey..92
Chapter 9..**103**
Life's Ups and Downs: Will Smith's Struggles and Triumphs.. 103
Chapter 10..**113**
A Legacy of Inspiration: Will Smith's Impact on Pop Culture.. 113

Chapter 1

A Boy from West Philadelphia

Once upon a time, in a bustling neighborhood of West Philadelphia, there lived a young boy named Will. He was not just any ordinary kid; he was a dreamer with a heart full of laughter and a head full of ideas. Will had a wild imagination, and his adventures often took him beyond the concrete streets and into the realms of his favorite superhero comic books.

Will lived in a cozy, brick house with his mom, dad, and three siblings. Their home was filled with the sounds of music, laughter, and the occasional playful argument over who got to use the TV remote. Will loved his family dearly, but he often felt like he was meant for something bigger. He had this funny feeling in his gut that he was destined for greatness, like the heroes he admired on the pages of his comics.

    One sunny afternoon, as Will was riding his bicycle down the block, he spotted a group of kids gathered around a makeshift stage in the park. Curious, he pedaled over, his heart racing with excitement. When he arrived, he found that the kids were putting on a talent show. Some were singing, others were dancing, and a few were even telling jokes that made everyone laugh until their bellies hurt.

Will watched in awe, his eyes sparkling with inspiration. "I can do that!" he thought. He had always loved making people laugh, and he was bursting with stories to share. So, with a deep breath, he stepped up to the stage, his knees shaking like jelly.

"Hi, everyone! I'm Will, and I'm here to tell you about my pet goldfish, Mr. Bubbles!" he announced, trying to sound brave. The crowd looked at him, some giggling, others curious. "You see, Mr. Bubbles thinks he's a shark! He swims around like he's about to attack... but really, he just wants food!"

The kids erupted in laughter, and Will felt a rush of joy. He continued with his silly stories, making funny faces and gestures that had the audience in stitches. For the first time, he felt like he belonged, like he was shining bright in a world that sometimes felt too big and overwhelming.

But just as Will was about to tell his best joke about a chicken crossing the road, something unexpected happened. A loud rumble echoed through the park, and the ground shook beneath their feet. The kids gasped and looked around, confused. Suddenly, a giant inflatable dinosaur, like something straight out of a movie, burst through the trees, its enormous green body wobbling as it approached.

"Run for your lives!" someone shouted, and chaos erupted. Kids were screaming and laughing at the same time, darting in every direction. Will's heart raced, but instead of running away, he felt a spark of bravery. "This is my moment!" he thought.

With a quick glance at the dinosaur, he decided to turn the chaos into comedy. "Hey, everyone! Don't worry! It's just Mr. Bubbles in a costume!" he shouted, waving his arms dramatically. The crowd paused, then burst into laughter again. Will's quick thinking had turned a scary situation into a hilarious one.

    As the inflatable dinosaur wobbled and flailed, it began to deflate, causing it to tip over and land with a soft thud on the grass. The kids cheered and clapped for Will, who had turned a moment of panic into a moment of joy. He realized that laughter was powerful; it could turn fear into fun and bring people together.

That day, Will learned something important: sometimes, life throws unexpected surprises your way, and it's up to you to decide how to handle them. With a little humor and a lot of heart, you can turn even the scariest moments into something wonderful.

Key Takeaway: Laughter can help us face our fears and bring people together, even in the craziest situations. Embrace your creativity and don't be afraid to shine!

Chapter 2

The Birth of DJ Jazzy Jeff and The Fresh Prince

In the bustling city of Philadelphia, where the streets hummed with the sounds of laughter, music, and the occasional skateboard whizzing by, two young dreamers were about to change the world of hip-hop forever. Will Smith, a charming teenager with a knack for making people laugh, and his best friend, DJ Jazzy Jeff, a wizard with turntables, were ready to take their talents to the next level.

Will was known for his smooth moves and quick wit. He could turn a dull moment into a comedy show, and he loved making people smile. Meanwhile, Jazzy Jeff, with his signature baseball cap and oversized headphones, could mix beats like nobody else. Together, they were a perfect match—like peanut butter and jelly or macaroni and cheese!

One sunny afternoon, while hanging out in Jeff's basement, the two friends decided it was time to create something special. "What if we made a rap group?" Will suggested, his eyes sparkling with excitement. "We could call ourselves DJ Jazzy Jeff and The Fresh Prince!"

Jazzy Jeff laughed, "That sounds awesome! But we need to write some songs first." And so, the duo got to work, scribbling down rhymes that blended Will's humor with Jeff's catchy beats. They wrote about everything from their crazy school adventures to the fun times they had hanging out with friends.

Their first big break came when they entered a local talent show. The competition was fierce, with other talented kids showcasing their skills in singing, dancing, and even magic tricks. But Will and Jazzy Jeff were determined to shine. They practiced day and night, perfecting their act until it was as smooth as a well-oiled machine.

On the day of the show, the auditorium buzzed with excitement. Will, dressed in a bright, colorful outfit, took the stage with Jazzy Jeff by his side, ready to drop some serious beats. The crowd was a mix of curious parents, energetic kids, and even a few skeptical teachers. Would they like what they were about to see?

    As the music started, Will launched into a rap that was funny and relatable. He joked about his parents, his homework, and even the weird things kids did at school. The audience erupted in laughter, and that laughter fueled his energy. Jazzy Jeff, meanwhile, was spinning records like a magician, making the crowd groove to the rhythm.

By the end of their performance, the audience was on their feet, clapping and cheering for the duo. They had done it! They won the talent show, and just like that, DJ Jazzy Jeff and The Fresh Prince were born. Their victory marked the beginning of an incredible journey filled with laughter, music, and friendship.

But success didn't come without challenges. As they began to perform more, they faced the pressure of keeping their act fresh and exciting. They had to come up with new songs and find ways to stand out. But instead of feeling stressed, they turned to their favorite source of inspiration: their everyday lives. They wrote about their experiences, their friendships, and the world around them.

    One day, while walking through their neighborhood, they noticed a group of kids playing basketball. They were laughing and having a great time, but there was also a little boy sitting alone on the sidelines. Will felt a tug at his heartstrings. "Hey, let's write a song about including everyone and being kind," he suggested. Jazzy Jeff nodded, and they got to work right away.

Their new song became a hit, spreading a message of friendship and acceptance. Kids everywhere started singing along, and DJ Jazzy Jeff and The Fresh Prince quickly became role models in their community. They showed everyone that music could bring people together, no matter their differences.

As they continued to rise in popularity, they learned that fame could be a double-edged sword. While they enjoyed performing and making people happy, they also faced challenges like balancing school, friendships, and their budding music careers. But through it all, they supported each other, proving that true friendship can weather any storm.

    With each performance, they not only entertained but also educated their audience about the importance of kindness, creativity, and believing in oneself. They were more than just a rap duo; they were a beacon of positivity in a world that sometimes felt chaotic.

Key Takeaway: Friendship and creativity can help you overcome challenges and inspire others. Always remember to include everyone and spread kindness, just like DJ Jazzy Jeff and The Fresh Prince!

Chapter 3

The Rise of The Fresh Prince of Bel-Air

Once upon a time, in the bustling city of Philadelphia, there lived a young man named Will Smith. Will was not your average teenager; he had a sparkling personality, a quick wit, and a knack for making people laugh. He was known for his amazing raps and dance moves, which made him the life of every party. But little did he know, his life was about to take a wild turn that would launch him into a whole new world.

One sunny afternoon, while Will was hanging out with his friends, he received an unexpected phone call. It was his long-lost Uncle Phil, who lived in the luxurious neighborhood of Bel-Air, California. Uncle Phil had heard about Will's talent and wanted him to come live with his family. Will's eyes widened with excitement. He had always dreamed of living in a fancy mansion with a pool and all the cool gadgets he had seen on TV. But there was one tiny catch—Uncle Phil wanted Will to leave his street-smart ways behind and embrace a more refined lifestyle.

As Will arrived in Bel-Air, he couldn't believe his eyes. The streets were lined with palm trees, and the houses were enormous, looking like they belonged in a fairy tale. Will stepped out of the car, wearing his favorite oversized T-shirt and sneakers, feeling like a fish out of water. His new home was a grand mansion with marble floors and chandeliers that sparkled like stars. "This is going to be epic!" he thought to himself, but he also wondered if he would fit in.

Will's new family included his Uncle Phil, a wise and serious lawyer; Aunt Viv, who was warm and nurturing; his snobby cousin Carlton, who loved to wear preppy clothes and dance like he was at a fancy ball; and his little cousin Ashley, who looked up to him like he was a superhero. Will was determined to make the best of his new life, even if it meant learning to navigate the world of the rich and famous.

On his first day at the prestigious Bel-Air Academy, Will strutted into school with his head held high. But as soon as he entered the classroom, he realized he was in for a challenge. His classmates wore designer clothes and spoke in a way that sounded like a different language. "What's up with all the 'like' and 'totally'?" he thought, trying to fit in while suppressing a giggle.

Will's first class was History, and his teacher, Mr. Dorsey, was a strict man who loved ancient civilizations. "Today, we're learning about Greek mythology," he announced. Will raised his hand, eager to share what he knew. "Hey, isn't Zeus the guy who throws lightning bolts? That's pretty cool!" The class erupted in laughter, and Mr. Dorsey couldn't help but crack a smile. "Yes, Will, but he also ruled over

Mount Olympus and was the king of the gods. You might say he had a shocking personality!"

Will's charm and humor quickly won over his classmates, but he still faced some challenges. Carlton often tried to outshine him with his perfect grades and fancy dance moves. The two cousins were like oil and water—Carlton loved classical music, while Will preferred hip-hop. One day, during a school talent show, Will decided to showcase his rapping skills. As he took the stage, he felt the adrenaline rush through him. "This is my moment!" he thought, remembering how he had rapped on the streets of Philly.

With a beat that made everyone's feet tap, Will launched into a hilarious rap about his life in Bel-Air. He joked about the differences between his old neighborhood and the posh lifestyle of his new friends. The audience roared with laughter, and even Carlton couldn't help but join in the fun. By the end of the performance, Will had stolen the show, proving that you could be yourself no matter where you were.

As the weeks went by, Will began to find his place in Bel-Air. He learned to appreciate the finer things in life, like fancy dinners and classical music, but he never lost his love for hip-hop and his street-smart ways. He also taught his family about his culture, introducing them to the joy of street games and the power of friendship.

One day, while hanging out with Ashley, Will noticed her looking sad. "What's wrong, little cousin?" he asked.

Ashley sighed, "I feel like I don't fit in at school. Everyone is so different." Will knelt down to her level and said, "Hey, being different is what makes you special! Just be yourself, and the right friends will come along." Inspired by his words, Ashley decided to embrace her uniqueness, and soon she found a group of friends who appreciated her for who she was.

As Will settled into his new life, he realized that while Bel-Air was fancy, the most important thing was being true to himself and the people he loved. He was becoming the Fresh Prince, not just in name but in spirit. He learned that laughter, friendship, and staying true to who you are could bridge any gap, no matter how big or small.

Key Takeaway: It's important to be yourself, no matter where you are. Embrace your uniqueness, and don't be afraid to share your culture and experiences with others. True friends will appreciate you for who you are!

Chapter 4

From Music to Movies: Will Smith's Hollywood Breakthrough

Will Smith stood on the stage, bright lights shining down on him like a thousand tiny suns. He was dressed in a colorful outfit that looked like it came straight from a funky 90s music video. The crowd cheered wildly, their voices blending into a wave of excitement that washed over him. He had just finished performing one of his hit songs, and the energy in the air was electric. But deep down, Will felt something tugging at his heart—a feeling that music, while fun, wasn't the only thing he wanted to do.

    You see, before Will became a superstar in Hollywood, he was known as "The Fresh Prince," a rap artist who could make anyone groove with his catchy beats and clever rhymes. He had a knack for storytelling through music, spinning tales about life in West Philadelphia, where he grew up. But as he stood there, microphone in hand, he couldn't shake the feeling that he was destined for something even bigger.

One day, while flipping through channels on his television, Will stumbled upon a show called "The Cosby Show." He watched as the characters laughed, cried, and shared their lives with the audience. It hit him like a lightning bolt: acting! Will realized he wanted to make people feel the same way, but through the magic of movies and television. He wanted to tell stories that would make people laugh, cry, and cheer, just like he did with his music.

But breaking into Hollywood wasn't going to be easy. Will knew he had to prove himself. So, he took a leap of faith and auditioned for a new TV show called "The Fresh Prince of Bel-Air." The show was about a street-smart kid from Philadelphia who moved to a fancy neighborhood in California to live with his wealthy relatives. It was a perfect fit for Will, who could relate to the character's adventures and misadventures.

The audition was intense! Will walked into the room, feeling a mix of nerves and excitement. He delivered his lines with a charm that could light up a room. The casting directors were impressed, and before he knew it, Will was cast as the lead.

He couldn't believe it! His dream was coming true, and he was about to become a household name.

As "The Fresh Prince of Bel-Air" hit the airwaves, it quickly became a sensation. The show was filled with humor, heart, and important lessons about family, friendship, and understanding different cultures. Will's infectious personality and comedic timing made audiences fall in love with him. Each episode was packed with laughter, but it also tackled serious topics like race, class, and growing up, showing kids that it was okay to talk about tough issues.

Will's transition from music to acting was seamless, but it wasn't without its challenges. Some people doubted him, thinking he would only be a rapper and nothing more. But Will was determined to prove them wrong. He worked hard, learned from every experience, and never lost sight of his goals. He even invited his old friends from the music world to guest star on the show, blending his two passions together in a way that felt natural and exciting.

As the seasons rolled on, "The Fresh Prince of Bel-Air" became one of the most beloved sitcoms of the 90s. Will's character, also named Will, faced hilarious situations, from dancing at fancy parties to getting into trouble with his strict Uncle Phil. Each episode was a new adventure, and viewers couldn't wait to see what would happen next.

But Will didn't stop there. He wanted to take his talent to the big screen. After the show wrapped up, he set his sights on Hollywood movies. He starred in action-packed films like "Independence

Day," where he fought aliens, and "Men in Black," where he teamed up with a mysterious agent to save the world from space invaders. His charisma and humor made him a star, and soon he was one of the highest-paid actors in Hollywood.

Will's journey from music to movies was filled with hard work, laughter, and a sprinkle of magic. He showed everyone that you could chase your dreams, no matter where you started. He believed that with passion and perseverance, anything was possible. And so, the boy from West

Philadelphia became a symbol of hope and inspiration for kids everywhere.

Key Takeaway: Pursuing your dreams may be challenging, but with hard work and determination, you can achieve great things, just like Will Smith did when he transitioned from music to acting!

Chapter 5

Facing Rejection and Overcoming Challenges

Will Smith stood backstage, heart pounding like a drum in a marching band. The bright lights flickered on the stage, and he could hear the audience laughing and clapping. But today wasn't about laughter; it was about facing something much scarier than a giant monster or a tricky math test—rejection.

He had auditioned for a role in a new movie, and the stakes felt as high as a roller coaster at the amusement park. The director, a grumpy man with a mustache that curled like a roller skate, had a reputation for being tough. Will could almost hear the director's voice echoing in his head: "You either bring it or you don't!"

Just a week ago, Will had been full of excitement. He practiced his lines in front of the mirror, making silly faces and pretending to be the character. He even wore his favorite bright yellow shirt, thinking it would make him stand out. "You got this, Will!" he told himself, imagining all the applause he would get. But when the day of the audition arrived, his confidence started to waver.

As he stepped onto the stage, Will felt like a superhero in a comic book, ready to save the day. But as he began his performance, he noticed the director scribbling something on a notepad. Will's heart sank. Was it a note about how great he was? Or was it a note about how he could improve?

After the audition, Will left the stage feeling like a deflated balloon. He had given it his all, but he couldn't shake the feeling that it wasn't enough. The next day, he received an email. "Thank you for auditioning, but we have decided to go in another direction."

"Another direction?" Will exclaimed, flopping onto his bed like a floppy fish. "What does that even mean?" He felt like he had been kicked by a giant foot.

But as he lay there, staring at the ceiling, he remembered something his mom used to say: "Every 'no' gets you closer to a 'yes.'" It was like a light bulb turned on in his mind. He realized that rejection was a part of life, just like getting a bad haircut or stepping in gum.

Determined not to let this setback defeat him, Will decided to take action. He picked up his phone and called his friend Jazzy. "Hey, Jazzy! Want to practice some scenes together?" he asked, his voice filled with newfound energy. Jazzy was always up for a challenge, and soon they were meeting every day after school, acting out funny skits and goofy characters.

They even created a hilarious scene where they pretended to be two talking cats who couldn't agree on what to have for dinner. "I want tuna!" Jazzy meowed dramatically, while Will, playing the other cat, replied, "No way! I'm craving pizza!" They rolled on the floor laughing, and in that moment, Will forgot all about his audition woes.

Weeks passed, and Will continued to practice. He learned new techniques, like how to project his voice and use body language to tell a story. With each silly skit, he became more confident. It was like training for a big race—each practice made him faster and stronger.

Then one day, while they were rehearsing, Will received another email. This time, it was an invitation to audition for a different movie! "This is it!" he shouted, jumping up and down like a pogo stick. He had faced rejection, but now he was ready to tackle this new opportunity head-on.

When the day of the new audition arrived, Will wore his lucky yellow shirt again. This time, he felt like a lion ready to roar. As he performed, he remembered all the fun he had with Jazzy and how much he had improved. The director, a kind lady with sparkly glasses, smiled and nodded as Will delivered his lines with confidence.

Afterward, Will left the stage feeling proud, no matter the outcome. He had faced his fears, learned from his mistakes, and discovered the power of friendship and practice. A few days later, he received the best news ever: he got the part!

As he celebrated with Jazzy, Will knew that rejection wasn't the end. It was just a stepping stone on the path to success. He learned that every challenge could be faced with a little humor, a lot of hard work, and the support of friends.

Key Takeaway: Rejection is a part of life, but it can help you grow stronger and better. Embrace challenges, learn from them, and remember that practice and friendship can help you overcome anything!

Chapter 6

The Box Office King: Will Smith's Blockbuster Success

Will Smith stood on the edge of Hollywood, a glimmering star in a galaxy of bright lights. He was not just any actor; he was a superhero of the silver screen! With his charming smile and quick wit, he could make you laugh, cry, or jump out of your seat in excitement. But what made Will truly special was his ability to connect with people, both on-screen and off. He had become the "Box Office King," ruling over the hearts of millions.

One sunny afternoon, Will was in his home studio, surrounded by colorful posters of his most famous movies. There was "Men in Black," where he played Agent J, a cool alien-fighting secret agent with a flashy neuralyzer that could erase memories. Then there was "Independence Day," where he saved the world from aliens with his quick thinking and bravery. Each movie was a piece of his legacy, a testament to his hard work and determination.

As Will flipped through the pages of his script for his next blockbuster, he couldn't help but think about how he got to this point. He had started his career as a rapper, known as "The Fresh Prince." But he didn't just want to be famous; he wanted to tell stories that mattered. So, he jumped into acting, and his big break came when he starred in the TV show "The Fresh Prince of Bel-Air." It was a comedy about a street-smart kid from Philadelphia who moved to a fancy neighborhood in California. The show was hilarious, and it taught important lessons about family, friendship, and being yourself.

Will's charm and humor quickly caught the attention of movie producers. They saw his potential and offered him roles in action-packed films. One of his biggest hits was "Bad Boys," where he teamed up with Martin Lawrence to fight crime in Miami. The film was filled with fast cars, epic chases, and lots of laughs. Audiences loved it, and it made a ton of money at the box office! Will was officially a superstar.

But it wasn't just about the money for Will. He wanted to inspire others, especially kids. He believed that everyone has a story to tell, and he wanted to show young people that they could chase their dreams too. In his movies, he often played characters who faced challenges but never gave up. In "The Pursuit of Happyness," he portrayed Chris Gardner, a struggling salesman who fought against all odds to provide a better life for his son. This film was based on a true story and taught audiences the importance of perseverance and hard work.

As Will continued to rise to fame, he faced challenges along the way. There were moments when he doubted himself and wondered if he would ever succeed. But he remembered the lessons he learned from his family and friends. They always encouraged him to stay true to himself and never lose sight of his dreams. With that motivation, he pushed through the tough times, proving that even the Box Office King had to battle his own fears.

One day, while filming a new movie about ancient mythology, Will found himself in an unexpected situation. The set was designed to look like the mythical city of Atlantis, filled with beautiful underwater scenes and magical creatures. During a break, Will noticed a group of kids watching from the sidelines. They were mesmerized by the costumes and special effects. Will decided to take a break from his role and interact with them.

"Hey, what's up, future movie stars?" he called out with a grin. The kids giggled and waved, excited to see their hero in person.

"Did you know that Atlantis is a legendary city that was said to have sunk into the ocean? Some people believe it was a real place!" Will shared, his eyes sparkling with enthusiasm. The kids listened intently, their imaginations running wild with thoughts of underwater adventures and lost treasures.

"Maybe one day, you'll make a movie about it!" one brave kid shouted.

"Absolutely!" Will replied, his heart swelling with joy. "And if you ever want to be in a movie, just remember: work hard, stay focused, and never give up on your dreams!"

With that, Will returned to the set, feeling inspired by the kids' excitement. He knew that he had a responsibility to not only entertain but also to inspire the next generation of dreamers and doers.

As the filming wrapped up, Will thought about his journey and the lessons he had learned. He realized that success wasn't just about being the best or making the most money; it was about making a difference and encouraging others to chase their dreams.

And so, the Box Office King continued to reign, not just with his blockbuster hits, but with a heart full of kindness and a mission to inspire. With every laugh, every tear, and every thrilling moment on screen, he reminded everyone that they too could shine brightly in their own stories.

Key Takeaway: Success is not just about fame or money; it's about inspiring others and staying true to yourself. Always chase your dreams and never give up, no matter how tough things get!

Chapter 7

A Family Man: Will Smith's Personal Life and Relationships

Will Smith was not just a superstar; he was also a family man who cherished the people closest to him. His life outside of the big screen was filled with laughter, love, and sometimes a little bit of chaos. Will had a knack for making every moment special, whether he was filming a blockbuster movie or just hanging out at home with his family.

Will married actress Jada Pinkett in 1997, and together they created a family that was as entertaining as any Hollywood film. They had two children, Jaden and Willow, who were not just kids; they were creative powerhouses! Jaden, with his cool style and love for acting, made his mark in movies like "The Pursuit of Happyness," where he starred alongside his dad. Willow, on the other hand, took the music world by storm with her catchy hit "Whip My Hair." It was like the Smith family had their own superhero team, each member with unique talents and super skills!

One sunny Saturday, Will decided to throw a family talent show at their home.

He set up a stage in the backyard, decorated with colorful lights and streamers. "Welcome to the Smith Family Talent Extravaganza!" he announced, wearing a shiny top hat and a huge grin. The kids giggled as they saw their dad's goofy outfit. It was clear that he was ready to bring the house down with laughter.

Jaden kicked off the show with a rap performance that had everyone tapping their feet. He spun around, his voice smooth like chocolate, while Will cheered him on from the front row. "That's my boy!" he shouted, clapping enthusiastically. Next up was Willow, who took the stage with her guitar. She sang a song about friendship that made everyone feel warm and fuzzy inside. Even the family dog, a fluffy golden retriever named Ace, seemed to wag his tail in rhythm.

After the kids had their turn, it was Will's time to shine. He jumped onto the stage, his top hat slightly askew, and announced, "Ladies and gentlemen, prepare yourselves for the greatest dad dance you've ever seen!" He started busting out moves that were a mix of silly and surprisingly smooth. Everyone laughed, especially Jaden and Willow, who couldn't believe how funny their dad looked. It was a moment of pure joy, filled with laughter that echoed around the yard.

But the talent show was more than just fun and games. Will believed in the importance of family, and he made sure to teach his kids valuable lessons along the way. He often told them, "It's not just about being famous; it's about being kind and helping others." He encouraged Jaden and Willow to give back to their community, and they often volunteered together at local shelters and schools. This made them not just stars but also shining examples of compassion and generosity.

One day, during a family dinner, Jada brought up a new idea. "How about we start a family project?" she suggested. "Let's create a video series where we share stories about kindness and how to make the world a better place!" Will's eyes lit up. "That's a fantastic idea! We can call it 'The Smith Family Kindness Chronicles!'" The kids jumped in excitement, ready to brainstorm ideas.

As they worked on their project, they discovered stories of real-life heroes, people who had done incredible things to help others. They learned about Mahatma Gandhi, who taught the world about peace, and Rosa Parks, who stood up for what was right. These stories inspired them, and they realized that even small acts of kindness could create big changes.

Through their videos, they shared their adventures, whether it was helping a neighbor or cleaning up a park. They laughed, learned, and even made a few silly mistakes along the way, but they always supported each other. Will taught them that it was okay to fail sometimes, as long as they learned from it and kept trying.

    As the sun set on their backyard talent show, the Smith family gathered around a fire pit, roasting marshmallows and telling stories. Will looked at his family, his heart swelling with pride. "You know," he said, "being a family is the greatest adventure of all. We may be in the spotlight, but what truly matters is the love and support we give each other."

The night ended with a group hug, laughter, and a promise to always stick together, no matter what challenges they faced. Will Smith, the superstar, was also Will Smith, the devoted dad, and that was the role he cherished the most.

Key Takeaway: Family is about love, support, and sharing moments together. It's important to be kind and help others, just like Will Smith and his family did!

Chapter 8

The Pursuit of Happiness: Will Smith's Inspirational Journey

Will Smith stood at the edge of a bustling Los Angeles street, the sun shining brightly overhead, casting long shadows from the tall buildings. He had just wrapped up filming a new movie, and the excitement buzzed in the air like a swarm of bees. But today wasn't just about movies; it was about something much deeper—happiness.

As he walked down the street, he thought about how his journey began. Will wasn't just a famous actor; he was also a rapper and a producer. In the late 1980s, he started as "The Fresh Prince," a fun-loving teenager in a sitcom that made everyone laugh. But behind the scenes, he was learning valuable lessons about life, dreams, and happiness.

"Hey, Will! Over here!" shouted a group of kids from a nearby park, waving their arms excitedly. Will turned and smiled, his heart warming at their enthusiasm. He loved connecting with kids and sharing his story. He jogged over, ready to inspire.

"Did you know that I started with nothing?" he asked, kneeling down to their level. "I grew up in West Philadelphia, and life wasn't always easy. But I had a dream, and I worked hard to chase it!"

The kids listened intently, eyes wide as saucers. "What was your dream?" a girl named Mia asked, her voice filled with curiosity.

Will chuckled, "I wanted to be a superstar! But it wasn't just about fame. I wanted to make people happy. That's what really matters. You see, happiness isn't something you find; it's something you create!"

Suddenly, a loud crash echoed through the park. A nearby ice cream truck had overturned, spilling colorful ice cream everywhere! The kids gasped, and Will's eyes sparkled with mischief. "Looks like we have a sweet situation here! Let's help clean it up!"

With a burst of energy, Will led the kids toward the mess. They laughed and squealed as they scooped up the ice cream, making silly faces and tossing the gooey treats at each other. In the midst of the chaos, Will shared stories about his own childhood—how he would often play with friends, inventing games and finding joy in simple moments.

"Did you know that in ancient Greece, people believed in the concept of 'Eudaimonia'? It's a fancy word for happiness, but it means living a life of virtue and purpose!" Will explained, wiping ice cream off his face. "It's not just about having fun; it's about being the best version of yourself!"

As the ice cream cleanup turned into a fun game, Will noticed the kids' laughter echoed like music in the air. Happiness was contagious! He reminded them, "Sometimes, you have to create your own happiness, just like I did. When I was struggling, I would write raps and make people laugh. That helped me find joy even when things were tough."

Just then, a gust of wind blew through the park, sending ice cream cups flying. The kids erupted into giggles, and Will couldn't help but join in. "See? Happiness is everywhere, even in the messiest moments!"

After the ice cream was cleaned up, Will gathered the kids around. "Always remember this: Life is full of ups and downs. There will be challenges, but you can choose how to respond. Find what makes you happy and go after it! Whether it's acting, dancing, or helping others, pursue your happiness with all your heart."

The sun began to set, casting a golden glow over the park. Will waved goodbye to the kids, who were still buzzing with excitement. As he walked away, he felt a sense of fulfillment. He knew he had shared something special with them—a spark of inspiration.

And as he made his way back to his car, he thought about the importance of happiness. It wasn't just a feeling; it was a choice. A choice he had made time and time again, and one that he hoped to pass on to everyone he met.

Key Takeaway: Happiness is something you create through your actions and choices. Even when life gets messy, you can find joy in the little moments and pursue what makes you truly happy!

Chapter 9

Life's Ups and Downs: Will Smith's Struggles and Triumphs

Will Smith stood at the edge of a stage, the bright lights beaming down on him like a thousand suns. The crowd was roaring, their cheers echoing through the air, but deep down, Will felt a storm brewing inside. He was about to share his story, and it was a tale filled with both struggles and triumphs.

As he looked out at the sea of faces, he thought back to the early days of his life. Growing up in West Philadelphia, he was a kid with big dreams but faced many challenges. He remembered the time when he was just a teenager, trying to juggle school, friendships, and his passion for music. It was like trying to balance a stack of pancakes on a rollercoaster! One moment he was soaring high, and the next, he felt like he might tumble down.

In high school, Will had a knack for making people laugh. He was the class clown, cracking jokes and pulling pranks. But not everything was a laugh-fest. Will struggled with math, which felt like a monster hiding under his bed. He often stayed up late, trying to conquer those tricky equations. It was during these late-night study sessions that he learned an important lesson: persistence pays off. Just like a superhero who trains hard to save the day, Will learned that hard work could lead to success.

His big break came when he was cast in the television show "The Fresh Prince of Bel-Air." It was a dream come true! But, oh boy, did the journey have its ups and downs. One day, he was the star of a hit show, and the next, he faced the harsh reality of money troubles. Will had earned a fortune, but he also lost it all due to bad investments. It was like being on a rollercoaster that suddenly dropped into a dark tunnel. He had to dig deep and find the strength to rise again.

In the midst of his struggles, Will discovered the power of friendship. His co-stars became his family, and together they supported each other through thick and thin. They laughed, cried, and shared their dreams, reminding Will that he wasn't alone in his battles. He often said, "Surround yourself with people who lift you up," and he truly believed it. It was like having a team of superheroes ready to fight alongside him!

As Will navigated through the twists and turns of life, he also faced criticism. Some people doubted him and said he wouldn't make it in Hollywood. But instead of letting those words pull him down, he used them as fuel. He worked harder, practiced his craft, and turned his setbacks into comebacks. It was like being in a video game where every time you lose a life, you come back stronger and more determined to win.

Will's triumphs didn't stop there. He eventually became a famous movie star, known for his roles in blockbuster hits like "Men in Black" and "Independence Day." But even as he stood on the red carpet, dressed to the nines, he never forgot where he came from. He often shared his story with kids, reminding them that it's okay to stumble as long as you get back up. Life was a series of ups and downs, and it was important to embrace every moment.

One day, as he was filming a new movie, he found himself in a high-stakes scene. He had to jump from one building to another, and the stakes were sky-high. As he prepared for the jump, he remembered all the times he had faced challenges. With a deep breath, he leaped into the air, soaring like a bird. He landed safely, and the crowd erupted in applause. Will realized that just like in life, sometimes you have to take a leap of faith to achieve your dreams.

With every struggle, he learned valuable lessons about resilience, friendship, and believing in himself. Will Smith's journey was a testament to the idea that life is a wild ride, filled with ups and downs, but it's the way you handle those moments that truly matters.

Key Takeaway: Life is full of challenges, but with hard work, friendship, and a positive attitude, you can overcome anything. Remember, it's okay to stumble; what's important is to get back up and keep going!

Chapter 10

A Legacy of Inspiration: Will Smith's Impact on Pop Culture.

Will Smith stood on the stage, the bright lights shining down on him like the sun on a summer day. The crowd cheered wildly, waving signs that read "Fresh Prince Forever!" and "We Love Will!" He smiled, feeling the energy of his fans wash over him. Little did they know, this was not just another award show; it was a celebration of how one man could change the world of entertainment forever.

Will had started his journey as a young rapper, performing catchy tunes that made people dance and laugh. But he didn't stop there! He jumped into acting, landing a role in the hit TV show "The Fresh Prince of Bel-Air." In this show, he played a street-smart teenager from West Philadelphia who moved to a fancy neighborhood to live with his wealthy relatives. The show was filled with humor, family values, and even some serious lessons about life. It was like a rollercoaster ride—fun, exciting, and sometimes a little scary!

As the years went by, Will transformed into a movie superstar. He starred in blockbuster films like "Men in Black," where he wore a cool black suit and fought aliens, and "Independence Day," where he saved the world from an alien invasion. Kids everywhere looked up to him, wanting to be just like the charming and funny hero on the screen. Will had become a role model, showing that you could be talented, funny, and kind all at the same time.

But what really set Will apart was his ability to inspire others. He wasn't just a star; he was a mentor. He used his fame to encourage young people to follow their dreams, no matter how big or small. In interviews, he often said, "You can't be afraid to fail. You have to be willing to take risks!" These words echoed in the hearts of kids who dreamed of being actors, musicians, or even astronauts. Will made them believe they could achieve anything if they worked hard and stayed true to themselves.

One day, while filming a new movie, Will decided to visit a local school. The kids were buzzing with excitement, their eyes wide with disbelief. "Is that really him?"

whispered a girl named Mia. "The Fresh Prince? The guy from the movies?" When Will walked into the gym, the room erupted with cheers. He spent the day sharing stories, cracking jokes, and answering questions. "What's your favorite movie?" a boy shouted. Will grinned and replied, "I love them all! But remember, it's not just about the movie; it's about the message. Always find the lesson in every story!"

As he left the school, Will felt a sense of fulfillment. He knew he was making a difference. He was planting seeds of inspiration in young minds, just like a gardener tending to his flowers. The kids would carry those lessons with them, growing into strong, confident individuals ready to take on the world.

Will's impact on pop culture didn't stop with his acting and music. He was also a social media superstar! He used platforms like Instagram and TikTok to connect with fans, sharing funny videos, dance challenges, and motivational messages. He showed everyone that it was okay to be silly and have fun, even as an adult. "Life is too short to be serious all the time!" he often said, making people laugh while also encouraging them to embrace their true selves.

In every role he played, whether it was a superhero or a charming con artist, Will Smith left a mark. He taught us about friendship, love, and the importance of believing in yourself. He showed us that we could all be heroes in our own lives, even if we weren't wearing capes or fighting aliens.

As the award show came to a close, Will stood on the stage, holding his trophy high. The crowd roared with applause, but he knew the real reward was the inspiration he had given to others. He smiled, thinking about all the kids watching, dreaming big dreams, and ready to take on the world. "This is for you!" he shouted, pointing to the audience. "Never stop believing in yourselves!"

Key Takeaway: Will Smith teaches us that we can all be heroes in our own stories. By believing in ourselves, working hard, and inspiring others, we can make a positive impact on the world around us.

Dear Reader,

Thank you for choosing "Little Big Giant - Stories of Wisdom and Inspiration"! We hope this book has inspired and motivated you on your own journey to success.

If you enjoyed reading this book and believe in the power of its message, we kindly ask for your support. Please consider leaving a positive review on the platform where you purchased the book. Your review will help spread the message to more young readers, empowering them to dream big and achieve greatness. We acknowledge that mistakes can happen, and we appreciate your forgiveness.

Remember, the overall message of this book is the key. Thank you for being a part of our mission to inspire and uplift young minds.